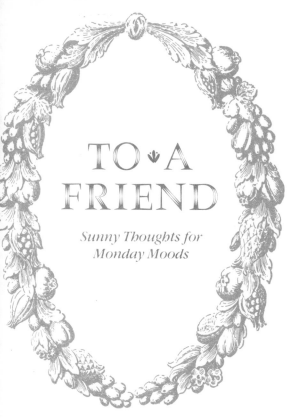

TO · A
FRIEND

*Sunny Thoughts for
Monday Moods*

By Jim Beggs

Designed by
Michel Design

PETER PAUPER PRESS, INC.
WHITE PLAINS · NEW YORK

Copyright © 1984, 1989
Peter Pauper Press, Inc.
202 Mamaroneck Avenue
White Plains, NY 10601
ISBN 0-88088-538-6
Library of Congress No. 88-63460
Printed in Hong Kong
5   4

TO A FRIEND

1

love is
one thing you can't keep
to yourself

2

before you put on a frown,
my friend,
make absolutely certain
there are no smiles available

3

do not be disappointed
if you have failed
to change the world;
be inspired
if you have lightened
even one person's burden
for one moment

4

if there is a gap
between past happiness
and future happiness,
bridge the present
with happiness remembered
and happiness anticipated

5

the mind should be
like a camera—
loaded with appreciation,
ready to capture
in full color
and in perfect focus
the essence
of each beautiful moment

6

luxury is
building tomorrows,
living todays,
and cherishing yesterdays

7

set a precedent for the day—
awaken with a smile!

8

however insufficient you may be,
love is the precise complement
to make you whole

9

impossibility
is an excuse—
never a reason

10

how can one be annoyed
by criticism?
if it is relevant,
learn from it;
if it is irrelevant,
ignore it—
but don't let pride
be the yardstick of relevance

11

as surely as
the sweetness of spring
shall follow
even the severest winter,
so shall
the sunshine of forgiveness—
ever pure and abundant—
disperse
the darkest night

12

a sparkling mountain brook
rushing from the Source—
tumbling,
tossing,
splashing,
and bubbling—
delivers an exuberant
Message
to all who will listen

13

the distance from failure
to success
is never longer
than the bridge of hope

14

to brighten someone else's life
is to increase the wattage
of your own

15

if I am wrong,
my friend,
please tell me
so I won't
reap a harvest of weeds

16

before you tell him
he is wrong,
remember:
you were wrong yesterday

17

anger:
when the spitting fire
is calm;
when the intense heat
is past;
when the flaming fury
is spent—
how wide
the trail of ashes?

18

many are the wonders
of the universe,
and many are those
that go unnoticed:
the little flower
off the path;
the pounding surf
on an unseen shore;
the inner glow
of someone's love—
so many wonders
tucked away

19

each new day is a symphony
orchestrated by
the sun, the sky,
the wind, the storms,
the earth;
and caring
provides the harmony,
while having a reason
to care
provides the melody

20

hope rises with the sun
every day;
don't forget—
it's even behind the clouds

21

forever
is the time-frame
of faith

22

the strongest foundation for
   one's life
and cornerstone for reality
is often
a dream

23

put on love in the morning
and wear it all day long

24

the color of a man's skin
makes no difference
to a blind man—
why is it
so many sighted men
cannot see?

25

the beauty of any one thing
is the threshold
to the wonder of the universe;
learn to appreciate a single tree,
any tree—
then turn into the forest deep
and saturate your soul!

26

as often as the sun sets,
my friend,
so shall it rise again;
for every twilight
of despair and disillusionment,
shall follow
a dawn of new hope
and new determination

there's something to be said
for trees and turtles—
one so upright and elegant,
one so horizontal and hunched;
one so sky-reaching,
one so ground-hugging;
one so firm yet flexible,
and one so unhurried yet
    persistent:
only trees and turtles
live longer than man

28

we are overwhelmed
far too often
by life's frustrations—
far too rarely
by its magnificence

29

the worst thing is
not that you said
what you said;
not that you did
what you did;
not that you failed,
faltered,
or fell short—
the worst thing is
that you hurt someone

30

sunset:
saving the best for last;
ending on a positive note;
salvaging;
climaxing;
celebrating—
day closes
with a sky to remember

faith is
truth beyond the grip of logic—
a silent knowing—
time refined to a purpose—
God focused into love—
and seeds eternal
gardened in the mind

32

anyone who can say
'love that eight o'clock
Monday morning!'
must be doing something right

33

money too often buys
people

continued happiness is the product
of optimism and imagination—
for optimism will inspire
the action toward a goal,
while imagination will save the day
(should the optimism prove unwarranted)
by ever identifying new goals
about which to be optimistic

35

if not God,
then how?
then why?
from what?
to where?

36

to find fulfillment,
my friend,
don't coexist with life—
embrace it!

standing on the seashore
watching the waves break,
I feel the tide
of exhilaration
sweeping over me—
lifting my spirits,
freshening my outlook,
and soothing my mind
with wave
after wave
of good feeling

38

beyond the sun—
beyond the stars—
beyond the galaxies—
beyond the universe—
within oneself—
Is

39

you can't see beyond
the bend in the road,
so watch where you're walking
in the meantime

40

don't make your life a game
of didn't do's
and shouldn't have's
moved randomly
by an unknown why

41

sunset is too frequently associated
with death;
but I would think of it rather
as the prelude
to yet another sunrise

42

morning:
one of the most beautiful words—
one of the most beautiful times—
forgiveness
for the day before;
hope
for the time to come;
and the promise
of another chance—
a fresh start.
morning:
one of God's
most beautiful gifts

43

if a person's actions are repugnant,
condemn the actions,
not the person;
whereas the actions cannot be undone,
the person may change

44

a person's worth
is not the value of what he has,
but rather
the potential of what he is

45

smile—
you must have done something right
at least once!

46

as I climb a mountain,
the mountain climbs
within me—
and from its summit
I survey
the magnificent vista
with wonder
and richness
filling up the chasms
in my soul

47

faith is the adhesive
binding
the uncertainty of now
with the inevitability
of forever

48

those who find happiness within
are destined
never to lose it;
but those who seek it elsewhere
are doomed
never to find it

49

how wonderful
to be alive;
how rich
to see another sunrise
and be healthy

50

love is an unlimited resource—
don't limit its use!

51

this day
and your life
are God's gifts to you—
so give thanks
and be joyful always!

52

whatever you do
in the name of Love,
my friend,
is never useless,
never harmful,
and, though not always seen
or recognized,
never without its rewards

53

one must have self-esteem
to the point of
feeling worthy of serving others,
but never to the point of
feeling worthy of being served

54

there are no miracles
for those who doubt their possibility;
but for those who believe—
truly believe—
all is possible

whatever you may have believed;
whatever you may have done;
and wherever you may be
in your life—
it's not too late
(it's never too late)
to change course
and begin anew

a fresh start,
a bright future,
and the wonderful peace
that passes all understanding
are yours for the taking,
now and forevermore

56

as a child of the Light,
may you always radiate to others
that illumination
which finds its expression in you
and you alone

we should never be so
  presumptuous
as to judge others
who do not believe
as we do

but if someone's way of life
is not filled with loving,
caring,
giving,
and sharing,
then perhaps our example
in these areas
may serve
to open the closed mind
and to soften the hardened heart

58

the more loving you become,
the better you will feel;
the better those around you will feel;
and the more you will be in
   harmony
with the Creator's richly
   fulfilling plan
for your life

59

never give up on anyone,
or believe that someone
is beyond help
or beyond hope—
no matter how cold,
negative, destructive,
or unloving
that person may be

for who is to say
that which is barren now
will not be fruitful next year?

60

what we say is important,
my friend,
for in most cases
the mouth speaks
what the heart is full of

but a pure heart is mirrored
not just by what we say,
but by all facets
of the life we live

61

a coming together
of the world's people
will occur
not as a unity of doctrine
or philosophy,
but rather
as a unity of Spirit

62

the more we focus on self-
  satisfaction
at the expense of others,
and the more we follow
hateful and hurtful plans
of our own devising,
the more frustration and despair
we inevitably create for ourselves

63

actions speak louder than words
about the true condition
of the heart,
and those in whose lives
the Spirit burns brightly
are often quiet souls
who carry out the work of love
without banner-waving

64

putting love on your lips
is of little value
unless it also lives
within your heart

65

the more people who experience
peace within,
the closer we are
to the world's peace, as well

let us, then,
pray for our friends
and our enemies
that all may find the inner peace,
so that one day—
in this life as well as the next—
all may live in harmony

we tend to remember
our own virtues
and other people's faults,
while overlooking
our own weaknesses
and other people's good points

for variety,
let's try the opposite today—
it might be enlightening!

67

never think of yourself
as useless,
worthless,
or having no purpose;
for whoever you are,
and whatever you are,
you are unique

and you can be assured
there is at least one thing—
however small—
that you and you alone can do
to make this world a better place

68

when your heart is loving,
my friend,
you feel the presence
of the Spirit
that lives within you

and those around you
reap the benefits
of your patience,
your kindness,
your caring,
and your joyfulness